Nourishing Neurodiversity

Simple Recipes to Nourish Your Body and Mind

Livia Sara

ISBN 979-8-9875398-6-6
eISBN 979-8-9875398-3-5

Photography by Livia Sara
Book Cover by Livia Sara and Mae van Aarsen

For more information, visit www.livlabelfree.com

Download my free guide!

To say thanks for buying my book, I'm giving you my exclusive guide 100% FREE!

In this guide, you'll find 5 strategies for navigating the kitchen from a neurodiversity-affirming and anti-diet perspective.

www.livlabelfree.com/kitchenhacks

This book is dedicated to all members of the neurodivergent community and their loved ones. You are unique and deserve to nourish yourself in a way that makes you happy <3

CONTENTS

INTRODUCTION

To be honest, I don't think I've ever followed a recipe from a cookbook before. In fact, I don't think I've ever followed a recipe *period*. So, why on Earth did I write a cookbook?! Because it's the single book I *would* follow a recipe from! And not just because they're my own recipes, but because they're *your* recipes, too. I explain what I mean below, but first, a little about me!

Growing up, I was an incredibly picky eater. From the moment I could eat solid food until the age of eleven, my diet consisted almost solely of sugary cereal in the morning, a bagel with cream cheese or a peanut butter & jelly sandwich for lunch, and macaroni & cheese with chicken nuggets and broccoli for dinner. Luckily, I wasn't too picky in the dessert department!

I acquired a love for baking around the age of seven, whipping up endless cookies, brownies, and cakes, then selling them along with lemonade in front of my house. To this day, my dad says those lemonade stands and bake sales were the start of my entrepreneurial journey! I even sold my symmetrical rainbow drawings at one point, too.

In fifth grade, I started learning about nutrition. My whole class would also be assessed on fitness capabilities starting that year. My literal thinking and perfectionistic mindset caused me to take each and every health "recommendation" to the deepest point in my heart, as I believed I would jeopardize my well-being if I didn't. I became obsessed with food, exercise, and everything that had to do with "health." At the age of eleven, I was diagnosed with anorexia and depression.

In the years that followed, I was forced in and out of treatment. I would act as the "perfect patient" during my stay, then spiral back into my routine ways as soon as I was released. I secretly exercised, hid food, manipulated my weight, and told my therapists what I knew they wanted to hear.

It wasn't until I walked all the way home from an inpatient clinic in the middle of the night, that one of the "best" psychiatrists in the country said the words that almost ended my life: *You're just going to have to accept the fact that you're never going to get better."*

I was tossed out of the treatment system with the labels "too complex," "manipulative," and "non-compliant," among others. The day I was given up on was also the day I lost all hope. Up until that time, treatment had been a game for me. I had done everything to manipulate the system, simply wanting to prove that no one could tell me what to do. But now? There was no more manipulation that could be done. I had been given up on…how was I supposed to rebel against that?

I continued to struggle for several years after that discouraging statement. Part of me wanted to recover and believed a better life was possible, while a seemingly stronger part of me couldn't let go of the rituals and routines that made me feel safe. Motivated by a desire to recover while being held back by the familiarity of my disorder, I started a "recovery" Instagram account. No one in my direct environment understood what I was going through, and I was desperate for connection. I craved support and understanding, and believed I would find it if I started opening up in the same way other accounts were.

Every day, I posted on Instagram. I shared my deepest, darkest thoughts in elaborate captions underneath pictures of my culinary creations. It was during this time that my passion for food was re-lit.

As I continued to evolve on my journey towards full recovery from an eating disorder, I learned more about food and what it really meant to eat healthily. It didn't mean restricting foods or food groups, or even striving for "balance." It meant living aligned with my unique body and its needs – it meant living label-free.

Almost a decade after being diagnosed with an eating disorder, I discovered I am autistic. If my journey to recovery from an eating disorder was like baking a cake, my autism discovery was the cherry on top. It allowed me to embrace myself fully, without needing to fight the very traits every eating disorder "professional" told me to get rid of. It allowed me to nourish my body without judgment. It allowed me to create and share recipes with pride rather than fear.

Ever since my autism discovery, my passion for neurodiversity and nutrition continues to grow. Understanding how the mind and gut are connected, and how you can improve your mental health by supporting your physical health, fascinates me beyond words. Learning how tailoring your intake to your specific needs and preferences can amplify your quality of life, astounds me beyond belief. And most importantly, embracing the label-free lifestyle – a lifestyle in which I can be the most authentic version of myself – has taught me how joyful life can be.

Through the following recipes, I hope to inspire and empower you and your loved ones to live and love that life. Although I do not follow any specific diet or labeled lifestyle, all of the recipes in this book are 100% vegan, gluten-free, soy-free, and nut-free. Many neurodivergent individuals are sensitive or intolerant to specific foods, so I have strived to accommodate all lifestyles to the best of my knowledge and ability.

You will also find executive functioning tips and health information throughout, as I believe nourishment starts with awareness of yourself and how your body works.

Lastly, every recipe in this book can be customized to fit your unique needs. I can't follow most recipes (or rather, I *won't* follow most recipes) because there's often an aspect I don't agree with – either an ingredient I don't have on hand, a step that's too complicated, or a texture that clashes with my personal preferences. For this reason, you will find arrows with suggestions for recipe-specific substitutions, as well as notes on how to customize the recipes to align with your needs.

Here's to nourishing neurodiversity!

XO,

Liv

INGREDIENTS & EQUIPMENT

While each recipe is unique and calls for different ingredients and equipment, I want to share a few staples that you'll find over and over in this book! Where appropriate, I have linked my favorite brands and any discount codes I have :) You can find specific ingredient substitutions in the recipes themselves.

Nuzest Clean Lean Protein:

Nuzest Clean Lean Protein is a 100% plant-based protein powder made from European golden peas. Unlike most vegan protein powders that are gritty and taste earthy, Nuzest's patented water-based processing technique results is a silky-smooth texture. They have a wide range of delicious flavors and the recipes in this book call for either vanilla or chocolate. However, feel free to switch things up with different protein flavors! **Visit livlabelfree.com/nuzest to snag major Nuzest discounts!**

Flours, Grains, + Legumes:

- Plantain Flour
- Coconut Flour
- Gluten-Free All-Purpose Flour (can always sub regular wheat flour if not gluten-free)
- Tigernut Flour (can always sub almond flour if not nut-free)
- Chickpea Flour
- Canned Chickpeas
- Canned Black Beans
- Dry Lentils
- Rolled Oats
- Rice
- Quinoa

Leaveners:

- Baking Powder
- Baking Soda

Sweeteners:

- Applesauce
- Maple Syrup (can always sub another sticky sweetener such as honey or agave)
- Sugar
- Dates (can always sub other dried fruit such as raisins or prunes)

Seeds:

- Chia Seeds
- Ground Flaxseed
- Sunflower Seeds
- Tahini

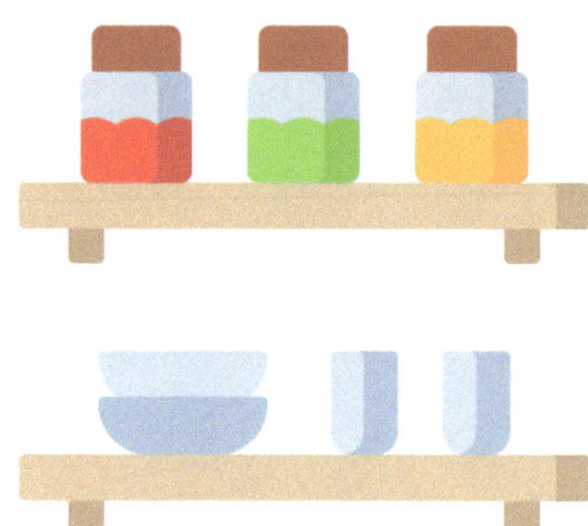

Oils, Extracts, and Spices:

- Coconut Oil
- Olive Oil
- Vanilla Extract
- Salt & Pepper
- Nutritional Yeast Flakes
- Ground Cinnamon
- Ground Nutmeg
- Ground Ginger
- Ground Cloves
- Ground Turmeric
- Ground Cumin
- Ground Paprika

Chocolate and Cacao:

- Cacao Powder
- Cacao Butter
- Cacao Nibs
- White Chocolate

Fridge Staples:

- Dairy-free Milk
- Coconut Yogurt
- Lemon Juice
- Tomato Sauce
- Vegan Mince
- Vegetable Broth
- Tofu (if you are soy-free, there are incredible soy-free tofu brands available nowadays)

Produce:

- Sweet Potatoes
- Pumpkin or Squash
- Banana
- Zucchini
- Bell Peppers
- Eggplant
- Baby Spinach
- Celery
- Carrots
- Frozen berries

Equipment:

- Blender - I highly recommend a Vitamix. Although on the pricier side, it's an investment that'll last you a lifetime. Thanks to the tamper, you can use your Vitamix as both a blender and a food processor!
- Air Fryer - bakes in a fraction of the time it takes in the oven!
- Chocolate Molds to make homemade chocolate!

**Find links to my favorite equipment
at livlabelfree.com/equipment**

BASICS

Perfectly Baked Japanese Sweet Potatoes (2 ways!)

INGREDIENTS

- Desired amount of Japanese sweet potatoes (about 200-300g each)

INSTRUCTIONS

Air Fryer Method:

1. Using a fork, poke a few holes in the sweet potatoes and place in the air fryer basket. Bake at 400F/200C for 20-25 minutes or until the potatoes are fork-tender.

Oven Method:

1. Preheat oven to 400F/200C and prepare a baking sheet.
2. Using a fork, poke a few holes in the sweet potatoes and place on the baking sheet. Bake for 45-60 minutes or until the potatoes are fork-tender.

freezing baked sweet potatoes

Batch-baking and freezing sweet potatoes ensures you always have them ready to go! To freeze your baked sweet potatoes, simply remove the skin, cut into cubes, and arrange evenly in an airtight container. Use as needed in soups, stews, curries, and in my Sweet Potato Smoothie Bowl on page 34!

Homemade Pumpkin Purée

Prep Time: 15 minutes

Cook Time: 30 minutes

Total Time: 45 minutes

Yield: ~3 cups (750g)

INGREDIENTS

- 1 kabocha pumpkin or squash (~2 pounds or 1kg)

INSTRUCTIONS

1. Preheat oven to 400F/200C and prepare a baking sheet.
2. Using a large, sharp knife, slice the pumpkin in half and scoop out the seeds and stringy insides.
3. Place pumpkin halves, cut side down, on the prepared baking sheet. Bake until very soft or until a fork pierces easily into the pumpkin. Depending on the size of your pumpkin, this can take anywhere between 30-45 minutes.
4. Remove from the oven and allow the pumpkin to cool on the baking sheet. Transfer pumpkin halves to a food processor or blender, and blend until smooth. You can choose to blend both skin and flesh to retain all of the nutrients, or remove the skin for a smoother purée.
5. Store pumpkin purée in a sealed container in the fridge for up to 5 days, or in the freezer for several months.

Making your own pumpkin purée at home is easy as pie! This simple recipe teaches you how to roast, purée, and store homemade pumpkin purée to use in your favorite pumpkin recipes. Once you know how to make pumpkin purée from scratch, you won't ever need to buy canned pumpkin again!

Plantain Flour Bread

Prep Time: 10 minutes

Cook Time: 40 minutes

Total Time: 50 minutes

Yield: 1 loaf

INGREDIENTS

- 3 cups plantain flour (360g)
- 1 teaspoon baking powder
- 1 teaspoon baking soda
- 1/2 teaspoon salt
- 2 tablespoons olive oil (30ml) *or other neutral oil*
- 1 tablespoon apple cider vinegar (15ml)
- 2 cups water (480ml)

lemon juice works too!

INSTRUCTIONS

1. Preheat oven to 375F/190C. Lightly grease a loaf pan with neutral oil or cooking spray and set aside.
2. In a large bowl, combine the dry ingredients.
3. Add the oil, vinegar, and water. Mix until you have a thick, yet smooth batter.
4. Transfer the batter to your prepared loaf pan and bake in preheated oven for 40-50 minutes or until a toothpick inserted in the center comes out clean.
5. Allow to cool completely before slicing.

WHAT IS PLANTAIN FLOUR?

An alternative to wheat flour, plantain flour is paleo and grain-free. Plantain flour is made from dry, green plantain slices by pulverizing the dried slices. It is prevalent in tropical regions of the world such as West Africa, South America, and the Caribbean. Because it can be directly substituted for conventional flour, plantain flour is used in similar ways, such as baking.

In addition to being a great gluten-free alternative in baking, plantain flour has many health benefits. It contains vitamins A, B, and C along with potassium, iron, phosphorus, and magnesium, which all help support muscle growth, heart health and function, and maintaining strong bones. Plantain flour can aid in promoting digestive health and help relieve digestive issues.

Plantain flour is high in resistant starch. This means it functions similarly to soluble fiber, an important component in digestion. High-resistant starches travel through the digestive tract and remain intact, helping to regulate overall digestion along with providing other health benefits (lower blood sugar and improve insulin sensitivity). Because they travel through the digestive system intact, these starches also feed the majority of the good bacteria in the colon. Ripe bananas contain less resistant starches, which is why green, unripe plantains are used to make plantain flour!

Sunflower Seed Butter

Prep Time: 10 minutes

Cook time: 10 minutes

Total Time: 20 minutes

Yield: ~3 cups (400g)

INGREDIENTS

- 3 cups raw sunflower seeds (400g)

INSTRUCTIONS

1. Preheat oven to 350F/180C and line a baking sheet with parchment paper.
2. Spread sunflower seeds evenly on a baking sheet and toast for 10 minutes, shaking halfway through.
3. Pour sunflower seeds into a high-power blender (preferably Vitamix) and blend on high, using the tamper to press the mixture into the blades. It should be creamy within a couple of minutes. Alternatively, you can use a food processor, but it will take longer.
4. Transfer your homemade sunflower seed butter to resealable jars and enjoy!

DID YOU KNOW?

Sunflower seeds provide tryptophan-rich proteins with the potential to protect against depression.

Easy Chia Jam (just 2 ingredients!)

Prep Time: 5 minutes

Cook Time: 5 minutes

Total Time: 10 minutes

Yield: ~1/4 cup (60g)

INGREDIENTS

- 1/2 cup berries of choice (60g)
- 1/2 tablespoon chia seeds (6g)
- 1 tablespoon water (15ml)

INSTRUCTIONS

1. Add berries, chia seeds, and water to a small saucepan. Bring to a gentle boil over low heat.
2. Once the water starts bubbling, start mashing the berries with a fork. Continue to mash the berries and stir the mixture until there are no more large chunks.
3. Allow the mixture to simmer for 5-7 minutes, or until a jammy consistency is reached.
4. Serve the jam warm (my favorite way!) on toast or oats, or store in the fridge for up to 5 days.

2-ingredient 100% Dark Chocolate

Prep Time: 10 minutes

Cook Time: 5 minutes

Total Time: 15 minutes

Yield: 2 small bars

INGREDIENTS

* 50g cacao butter
* 50g cacao powder

INSTRUCTIONS

1. Prepare a double boiler by adding water to a medium saucepan, and topping it with a heat-proof bowl that is slightly larger than the circumference of the pan. Bring the water to a gentle boil over medium-low heat.
2. Place the cacao butter in the bowl and allow it to melt, whisking occasionally to prevent scorching.
3. Once the cacao butter is fully melted, whisk in the cacao powder in small increments.
4. Continue heating and mixing until you have a mixture that resembles melted chocolate.*
5. Remove the pan from the heat and pour melted chocolate into your chocolate molds.
6. Set the chocolate in the fridge for at least 1 hour to set.

NOTES

*If you want to add any sweeteners, whisk them into the mixture at this step.

step 2

step 3

step 4

voilà!

customize it!

For extra flavors and textures, try adding in dried fruits, nuts, and/or seeds!

Sensory-friendly Hummus

Prep Time: 5 minutes

Total Time: 5 minutes

Yield: ~2 cups (500g)

INGREDIENTS

- 15 oz can chickpeas (240g drained weight)
- 1/4 cup tahini (60g)
- 2 tablespoons fresh lemon juice (30ml)
- 1/2 teaspoon baking soda
- 1/4 teaspoon salt
- 1/2 teaspoon ground cumin
- 1/4 cup cold water (60ml)
- 1 tablespoon extra virgin olive oil (15ml)

INSTRUCTIONS

1. Add all ingredients to a blender or food processor.
2. Blend on high until smooth and creamy.
3. Transfer hummus to a sealed container or jar. Keeps in the fridge for up to 5 days.

what makes this hummus sensory-friendly?

Most recipes for hummus (including store-bought varieties) include garlic, which can cause digestive issues in hypersensitive individuals. For this reason, you won't find it in this recipe! If you can tolerate garlic, feel free to add as desired.

Drippy Black Bean Hummus

Prep Time: 5 minutes

Total Time: 5 minutes

Yield: ~2 cups (500g)

INGREDIENTS

- 15 oz can black beans, liquid reserved (400g)
- 1/4 cup tahini (60g)
- 2 tablespoons fresh lemon juice (30ml)
- 1/2 teaspoon ground cumin
- 1 dash smoked paprika
- 1/4 teaspoon baking soda

INSTRUCTIONS

1. Add all ingredients to a blender or food processor.
2. Blend on high until smooth and creamy.
3. Transfer to a sealed container or jar. Keeps in the fridge for up to 5 days.

how can I use this recipe?

Made with black beans and super drippy, this Mexican twist on the classic hummus is perfect for salads, as a dip, or even as a creamy pasta sauce!

Lemon Tahini Dressing

Prep Time: 5 minutes

Total Time: 5 minutes

Yield: 1/2 cup (120g)

INGREDIENTS

- 1/4 cup tahini (60g)
- 2 tablespoons fresh lemon juice (30ml)
- 1 tablespoon olive oil (15ml) *or other neutral oil*
- 1 tablespoon water (15ml)
- 1 tablespoon maple syrup (15ml) *or another sticky sweetener such as honey or agave*
- Salt and pepper, to taste

INSTRUCTIONS

1. Add all ingredients to a jar and seal tightly with a lid.
2. Shake well and use as desired! Refrigerate any unused portion for up to 5 days.

What is tahini?

Tahini is a silky-smooth paste made from ground sesame seeds, making it an excellent alternative to nut butter. Sesame seeds are high in tyrosine and tryptophan, two amino acids that aid in the production of dopamine and serotonin in the brain.

BREAKFAST BOWLS

Vanilla Cauliflower Protein Oatmeal

Prep Time: 5 minutes

Cook Time: 10 minutes

Total Time: 15 minutes

Yield: 1 bowl

INGREDIENTS

- 1/2 cup rolled oats (40g)
- 1 scoop vegan vanilla protein powder (12-15g)
- 1/2 cup cauliflower rice (50g)
- 1 cup milk of choice (240ml)
- Optional: maple syrup and/or cinnamon for extra flavor

INSTRUCTIONS

1. Add all ingredients to a saucepan and mix well. Bring to a gentle boil over medium heat.
2. Reduce heat to low and allow oats to simmer until thick & creamy. Make sure to stir occasionally to prevent the oats from sticking to the bottom of the pan.
3. Transfer oats to a bowl and top with whatever you desire!

customize it!

Top your bowl with a combination of fruit + nuts/seeds for a complete breakfast that hits all the main food groups!

Banana Bread Oatmeal

Prep Time: 5 minutes

Cook Time: 10 minutes

Total Time: 15 minutes

Yield: 1 bowl

INGREDIENTS

- 1/2 cup rolled oats (40g)
- 1/2 tablespoon whole flaxseeds (6g)
- 1 scoop vegan vanilla protein powder (12-15g)
- 1/2 medium banana + *more for topping*
- 1 tablespoon nut/seed butter (15g) + *more for topping*
- cinnamon and sea salt, to taste
- 1-1/4 cup water (300ml)

INSTRUCTIONS

1. Add the oats, flaxseeds, and protein powder to a saucepan. Mash the banana and add it along with the nut/seed butter, cinnamon, salt, and water. Mix well.
2. Bring the mixture to a gentle boil over medium heat.
3. Once bubbling, reduce heat to low and allow porridge to simmer until thick and creamy.
4. Transfer to a bowl and top with whatever you desire!

DID YOU KNOW? Bananas are high in serotonin and vitamin B6, both of which can help boost your mood!

Chocolate Microwave Oatmeal

Prep Time: 5 minutes

Cook Time: 5 minutes

Total Time: 10 minutes

Yield: 1 bowl

INGREDIENTS

- 1/2 cup quick oats (40g)
- 1 scoop vegan chocolate protein powder (12-15g)
- 1 1/2 tablespoons cocoa or cacao powder (10g)
- 1/2 cup cauliflower rice (50g)
- 1/2 cup hot water (120ml)
- 1/4 cup milk of choice (60ml) *+ more, as needed*

INSTRUCTIONS

1. Add the oats, protein powder, cocoa powder, and optional veggies to a microwave-safe bowl.
2. Add the water and milk, stirring well to remove any clumps.
3. Microwave on HIGH for 1 minute. Remove from microwave, giving the oats a good stir. If they are too thick, add some more milk at this step.
4. Place back in the microwave for another 30 seconds or so, heating and stirring until desired consistency is reached.
5. Top with your favorites and enjoy!

Pumpkin Protein Oatmeal

Prep Time: 5 minutes

Cook Time: 10 minutes

Total Time: 15 minutes

Yield: 1 bowl

INGREDIENTS

- 1/2 cup rolled oats (40g)
- 1 scoop vegan vanilla protein powder (12-15g)
- 1/4 cup pumpkin purée (60g)
- 1/2 teaspoon pumpkin pie spice (see below)
- 1 cup milk of choice (240ml)
- Optional: maple syrup for extra sweetness

no pumpkin pie spice? no problem!

Simply add a dash of cinnamon, ginger, nutmeg, and cloves instead :)

INSTRUCTIONS

1. Add the oats, protein powder, pumpkin purée, spices, and milk to a saucepan. Whisk to combine and bring the mixture to a gentle boil over medium heat.
2. Once bubbling, reduce heat to low and allow oats to simmer until thick & creamy. Stir occasionally to prevent the oats from sticking to the bottom of the pan.
3. Transfer to a bowl and top with whatever you desire!

Spicy Turmeric ZOATS

Prep Time: 5 minutes

Cook Time: 10 minutes

Total Time: 15 minutes

Yield: 1 bowl

INGREDIENTS

- 1/2 cup rolled oats (40g)
- 1 tablespoon ground flaxseeds (7g)
- 1 scoop vegan vanilla protein powder (12g-15g)
- 1/2 cup shredded zucchini (50g)
- 1/4 teaspoon cinnamon
- 1/4 teaspoon ground turmeric
- Pinch black pepper
- 1 cup milk of choice (240ml)
- 1/4 cup water (60ml)
- Optional: maple syrup for extra sweetness

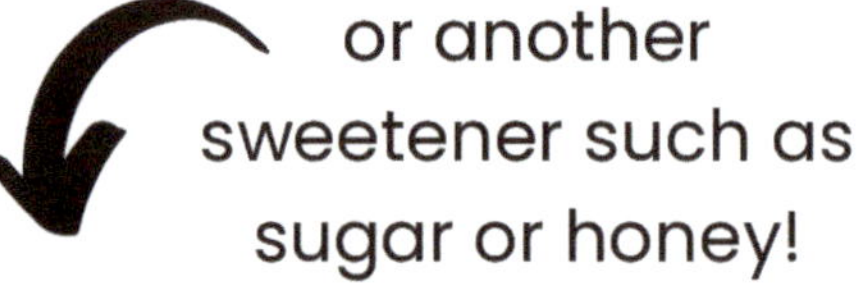

INSTRUCTIONS

1. Add oats, flaxseeds, protein powder, zucchini, spices, milk, water, and sweetener to a saucepan and mix well. Bring to a gentle boil over medium heat.
2. Once bubbling, reduce heat to low and allow oats to simmer until thick & creamy. Stir occasionally to prevent oats from sticking to the bottom of the pan.
3. Transfer to a bowl and top with whatever you desire!

What the heck are ZOATS?

Zucchini + oats = ZOATS! The addition of shredded zucchini is an excellent way to pack in extra veggies.

DID YOU KNOW?

Turmeric's most active compound is curcumin, a powerful anti-inflammatory that can soothe symptoms of joint pain. Unfortunately, curcumin is poorly absorbed into the bloodstream. When combined with black pepper (which contains the compound piperine), however, curcumin's bioavailability increases by approximately 2000%! That's why I recommend always adding a pinch of black pepper when cooking with turmeric :)

Easy Chia Pudding

Prep Time: 5 minutes

Total Time: 5 minutes

Yield: 1 bowl

INGREDIENTS

- 1 cup milk of choice (240ml)
- 3 tablespoons chia seeds (35g) *see below for substitution*
- 1 scoop vegan vanilla protein powder (12-15g)
- Optional: maple syrup and/or cinnamon for extra flavor

no chia seeds? no problem!

You can easily substitute equal amounts of whole flaxseeds for similar results. Both are high in fiber, omega-3s, and antioxidants!

INSTRUCTIONS

1. Add your milk to a sealable glass jar, followed by the chia seeds, protein powder, and any additional sweeteners or flavorings.
2. Tightly seal the jar with a lid and shake well.
3. Place in the refrigerator to thicken for at least 4 hours, or overnight. Top as desired and enjoy!

Sticky Brown Rice Pudding

Prep Time: 5 minutes

Total Time: 5 minutes

Yield: 1 bowl

INGREDIENTS

- 1/2 cup cooked brown rice (90g) *or sub white rice*
- 1/2 tablespoon chia seeds (6g)
- 1 scoop vegan vanilla protein powder (12-15g)
- 1/3 cup milk of choice (80ml)
- 1 tablespoon maple syrup (15ml)

INSTRUCTIONS

1. Add all ingredients to a bowl and mix well.
2. Enjoy cold or heat porridge (in the microwave or on the stovetop) until desired temperature is reached.
3. Top with your favorites and enjoy!

BROWN RICE vs. WHITE RICE

If you're reading this, you may have expected to find something along the lines of "brown rice is better than white rice"...but I'm here to remind you that no food is superior over another because ALL FOODS FIT into a balanced + healthy lifestyle! :)

Creamy Sweet Potato Breakfast Bowl

Prep Time: 5 minutes

Total Time: 5 minutes

Yield: 1 bowl

INGREDIENTS

- 1 medium sweet potato *baked, see notes*
- 1 scoop vegan vanilla protein powder (12-15g)
- 1/3 cup milk of choice (80ml)
- Optional: maple syrup and/or cinnamon for extra flavor

INSTRUCTIONS

1. Add all ingredients to a food processor or blender and mix until smooth. Top as desired and enjoy!

NOTES

See my recipe for Perfectly Baked Japanese Sweet Potatoes in the oven or air fryer on page 10!

DID YOU KNOW?

Sweet potatoes are high in fiber and antioxidants, both of which support gut health!

Pumpkin Pie Breakfast Bowl

Prep Time: 5 minutes

Total Time: 5 minutes

Yield: 1 bowl

INGREDIENTS

- 1 cup pumpkin purée (240g) *for homemade, see notes*
- 1 scoop vegan vanilla protein powder (12-15g)
- 1/3 cup milk of choice (80ml)
- Dash pumpkin pie spice (see page 27 for substitution)

INSTRUCTIONS

1. Add all ingredients to a bowl and mix until smooth. Top as desired and enjoy!

NOTES

See my recipe for Homemade Pumpkin Purée on page 12!

Use green-skinned kabocha squash for a green bowl!

Sweet Potato Smoothie Bowl

Prep Time: 10 minutes

Total Time: 10 minutes

Yield: 1 bowl

INGREDIENTS

- 1 cup milk of choice (240ml)
- 1 scoop vegan vanilla protein powder (12-15g)
- 1 cup frozen sweet potato chunks (120g) *see notes*
- 1/2 cup frozen strawberries (60g)
- 1/2 cup frozen blueberries (60g)

NOTES

To learn how to best freeze sweet potatoes, see my recipe for Perfectly Baked Japanese Sweet Potatoes on page 10!

INSTRUCTIONS

1. Add all ingredients to a high-speed blender (preferably a Vitamix) and blend until smooth and creamy.
2. Transfer smoothie to a bowl and add desired toppings!

Banana Berry Smoothie Bowl

Prep Time: 10 minutes

Total Time: 10 minutes

Yield: 1 bowl

INGREDIENTS

- 2/3 cup milk of choice (160ml)
- 1 scoop vegan vanilla protein powder (12-15g)
- 1/2 tablespoon chia seeds (6g)
- 1/2 frozen banana (60g)
- 1/2 cup frozen strawberries (60g)
- 1/2 cup frozen blueberries (60g)

INSTRUCTIONS

1. Add all ingredients to a high-speed blender (preferably a Vitamix) and blend until smooth and creamy.
2. Transfer smoothie to a bowl and add desired toppings!

STRUGGLING WITH DIGESTIVE ISSUES?

Smoothies and other pureed foods are a great way to give your digestive system a break. By blending the food before consuming it, your body doesn't have to work as hard!

Creamy Quinoa Chia Porridge

Prep Time: 5 minutes

Total Time: 5 minutes

Yield: 1 bowl

INGREDIENTS

- 1/2 cup cooked quinoa (90g)
- 1/2 tablespoon chia seeds (6g)
- 1 scoop vegan vanilla protein powder (12-15g)
- 1/3 cup milk of choice (80ml)
- Optional: maple syrup and/or cinnamon for extra flavor

INSTRUCTIONS

1. Add all ingredients to a bowl and mix well.
2. Enjoy cold or heat porridge (in the microwave or on the stovetop) until desired temperature is reached.
3. Top with your favorites and enjoy!

executive functioning tip!

Reduce the overwhelm by cooking one big pot of quinoa at the start of the week, then use it in different recipes such as this porridge!

Productive Toast (endless variations!)

tell me more!

WHAT IS PRODUCTIVE TOAST?

I'm so glad you asked! I came up with the term "productive toast" as I was brainstorming how I could group the foods bread, squash, and sweet potato together. The term "productive" relates to squash and sweet potato being "produce," and "toast" obviously refers to bread! Better yet, the duo lends quite a remarkable hand in the semantics department, because this breakfast truly sets your day off to be productive! ;)

So why group produce and bread together in the first place? Because both "categories" of food serve as the base for this infinitely customizable recipe! Here's how we do it:

HOW TO MAKE PRODUCTIVE TOAST

1. For the base, choose from
   - Bread (toasted or not, it's up to you!)
   - Baked sweet potato
   - 1/2 small baked butternut squash
2. Top your base with yogurt (or if using squash, *fill* your base!)
3. Top your yogurt with fruit of choice (chia jam, banana coins, sautéed cinnamon apples or pears are some of my personal favorites)
4. Finish it all off with a drizzle of nut/seed butter and anything else you desire!

TOPPING INSPO!

The sky is the limit when it comes to toppings! Some of my favorite additions to productive toast include: granola, chocolate chips, cacao nibs, cereal, and dried fruit.

variation inspiration!

whole-grain toast + thick yogurt, chia jam, and a nut/seed butter drizzle

whole-grain toast + thick yogurt, banana coins, and a nut/seed butter drizzle

baked Japanese sweet potato + thick yogurt, chia jam, and a nut/seed butter drizzle

SINGLE-SERVE CAKES

Fluffy Chickpea Flour Pancakes

Prep Time: 10 minutes

Cook Time: 10 minutes

Total Time: 20 minutes

Yield: 5-6 pancakes

INGREDIENTS

- 1/3 cup chickpea flour (45g)
- 1/2 teaspoon baking powder
- 1 scoop vegan vanilla protein powder (12-15g)
- 1/3 cup milk of choice (80ml) *+ more, as needed*
- 1x recipe homemade chia jam (p. 17) + nut/seed butter for topping

INSTRUCTIONS

1. Add dry ingredients to a small mixing bowl and whisk to combine.
2. Add the milk, mixing until you have a smooth, yet thick batter (a thick batter is the key to fluffy pancakes!).
3. Heat a skillet or griddle on medium heat. Once hot, grease with oil, butter, or cooking spray.
4. Spoon batter onto hot, greased surface, cooking until pancakes slightly bubble and edges are lightly golden.
5. Carefully flip pancakes, and cook until browned on the underside, about 1-2 minutes.
6. Repeat with remaining batter. Transfer to a plate, top with chia jam and nut/seed butter, and enjoy!

Blueberry Oatmeal Protein Pancakes

Prep Time: 10 minutes

Cook Time: 10 minutes

Total Time: 20 minutes

Yield: 5-6 pancakes

INGREDIENTS
- 1/2 cup oat flour (60g)
- 2 tablespoons ground flaxseed (14g)
- 1/2 teaspoon baking powder
- 1/2 teaspoon cinnamon
- 2 scoops vegan vanilla protein powder (25-30g)
- 1 cup milk of choice (240ml)
- 1/2 cup blueberries (60g) *fresh or frozen*

INSTRUCTIONS
1. Add dry ingredients to a small mixing bowl and whisk to combine.
2. Mix in the milk. Let batter sit for about 5 minutes to thicken (the flaxseeds will soak up the liquid!).
3. Heat a skillet or griddle on medium heat. Once hot, grease with oil, butter, or cooking spray.
4. Spoon batter onto hot, greased surface, topping each pancake with a couple of blueberries. Cook until pancakes slightly bubble and the edges are lightly golden.
5. Carefully flip pancakes, and cook until browned on the underside, about 1-2 minutes.
6. Repeat with the remaining batter. Transfer to a plate, top with your favorites, and enjoy!

Plantain Flour Pancakes (just 3 ingredients!)

Prep Time: 10 minutes

Cook Time: 10 minutes

Total Time: 20 minutes

Yield: 5-6 pancakes

INGREDIENTS

- 1 cup plantain flour (120g)
- 2 teaspoons baking powder
- 1 cup milk of choice (240ml)

switch up your sensory experience!

Use the same ingredients and adjust instructions for waffles to explore different textures with the trust of a familiar recipe!

INSTRUCTIONS

1. Whisk together the dry ingredients. Mix in the milk. Let the batter rest for about 5 minutes so your pancakes will be nice and fluffy.
2. Meanwhile, heat a skillet or griddle on medium heat and grease with butter, oil, or cooking spray.
3. Spoon batter onto your hot skillet, cooking pancakes for 1-2 minutes, or until small bubbles form on the surface.
4. Flip, and cook for an additional 1-2 minutes, or until golden brown.
5. Repeat with remaining batter and serve with toppings of choice!

TIPS FOR THE PERFECT MUG CAKE

#1 mixing your ingredients

When mixing your batter, be sure to incorporate the dry ingredients at the bottom of the mug. If not, you'll end up with clumps of dry flour, which will obviously lead to sub-par results!

#2 microwave power level

When microwaving your mug cake, I recommend adjusting the power of your microwave to medium, or 500W. Microwaving the mug cake at medium power better simulates baking in a regular oven because the heat will be lower and more consistent. If you tried zapping your cake on HIGH instead, the texture would turn out gummier, and the top of the cake would be nearly overdone while the center would be raw. And we don't want that, do we? So, be sure to stick with medium or low power :)

#3 better safe than sorry!

If you're unsure how long to microwave your mug cake in your specific microwave, I recommend starting on the lower time end (1 minute), then microwaving in 15-second increments until done. You can always cook longer, but you can never go back if it's overcooked!

Double Chocolate Mug Cake

Prep Time: 5 minutes

Cook Time: 2 minutes

Total Time: 7 minutes

Yield: 1 cake

INGREDIENTS

- 1 1/2 tablespoons plantain flour (12g)
- 1 tablespoon coconut flour (7g)
- 1 1/2 tablespoons cocoa powder (10g)
- 1/2 teaspoon baking powder
- 1 scoop vegan chocolate protein powder (12-15g)
- 1 tablespoon nut/seed butter of choice (15g)
- 1/3 cup milk of choice (80ml)
- Chocolate chips or chunks, for topping

INSTRUCTIONS

1. In a microwave-safe mug, whisk together the flours, cocoa powder, baking powder, and protein powder.
2. Add the nut/seed butter and milk, mixing until you have a smooth batter (see my tips on page 45!).
3. Top with chocolate, then microwave at medium power for approximately 2 minutes, or until set (see tips!).
4. Allow to cool for at least 2 minutes and enjoy!

Cinnamon Roll Mug Cake

Prep Time: 5 minutes

Cook Time: 2 minutes

Total Time: 7 minutes

Yield: 1 cake

INGREDIENTS

- 2 tablespoons plantain flour (16g)
- 1 tablespoon coconut flour (7g)
- 1/4 teaspoon baking powder
- 1/2 teaspoon cinnamon
- 1 scoop vegan vanilla protein powder (12-15g)
- 1 tablespoon nut/seed butter of choice (15g)
- 1/3 cup milk of choice (80ml)
- Coconut yogurt + coconut flakes, to top (optional)

INSTRUCTIONS

1. In a microwave-safe mug, whisk together the flours, baking powder, cinnamon, and protein powder.
2. Add the nut/seed butter and milk, mixing until you have a smooth batter (see my tips on page 45!).
3. Microwave at medium power for approximately 2 minutes, or until set (see tips!).
4. Allow to cool for at least 2 minutes.
5. Top with yogurt and coconut flakes, and enjoy!

Quadruple Chocolate Waffles

Prep Time: 10 minutes

Cook Time: 5 minutes

Total Time: 15 minutes

Yield: 4 waffles

INGREDIENTS

- 1 1/2 tablespoons plantain flour (12g)
- 1 tablespoon coconut flour (7g)
- 1 1/2 tablespoons cocoa powder (10g)
- 1/2 teaspoon baking powder
- 1 scoop vegan chocolate protein powder (12-15g)
- 1 teaspoon melted coconut oil (5g)
- 1/3 cup milk of choice (80ml)
- Chocolate chips + cacao nibs, for topping

INSTRUCTIONS

1. Preheat waffle iron according to manufacturer's instructions.
2. In a bowl, whisk together the dry ingredients.
3. Add the oil and milk, mixing until you have a smooth, yet thick batter.
4. Grease preheated waffle iron on all sides, and scoop batter onto the hot surface.
5. Close iron and cook for 3-5 minutes, or until done.
6. Top with chocolate and any other desired toppings!

Berry Coconut Waffles

Prep Time: 10 minutes

Cook Time: 5 minutes

Total Time: 15 minutes

Yield: 4 waffles

INGREDIENTS

- 3 tablespoons plantain flour (23g)
- 1 tablespoon coconut flour (7g)
- 1/2 teaspoon baking powder
- 1 scoop vegan vanilla protein powder (12-15g)
- 1 teaspoon melted coconut oil (5g)
- 1/4 cup coconut yogurt (60g)
- 1/3 cup water (80ml)
- Berries, nut/seed butter, and yogurt, for topping

INSTRUCTIONS

1. Preheat waffle iron according to manufacturer's instructions.
2. In a bowl, whisk together the dry ingredients.
3. Add oil, yogurt, and water, mixing until you have a smooth, yet thick batter.
4. Grease preheated waffle iron on all sides, and scoop batter onto the hot surface.
5. Close iron and cook for 3-5 minutes, or until done.
6. Top with desired toppings and enjoy!

SAVORY

Easy Vegan Chili

Prep Time: 10 minutes

Cook Time: 20 minutes

Total Time: 30 minutes

Yield: 2-4 servings

INGREDIENTS

- 2 tablespoons olive oil (30ml)
- 1 yellow onion, chopped (omit if sensitive to onion)
- 1 large red bell pepper, chopped
- 1 large yellow or orange bell pepper, chopped
- 1 medium eggplant, cubed (or sub another bell pepper)
- 15 oz pack vegan mince (400g)
- 1/2 teaspoon paprika powder
- 2 teaspoons ground cumin
- 2 teaspoons ground coriander
- 1/2 teaspoon chili powder (adjust amount depending on heat preference)
- salt and pepper (to taste)
- 2 cups tomato sauce (480ml)
- 15 oz can black beans (240g drained weight) *can sub another bean such as kidney or cannellini*

INSTRUCTIONS

1. Heat oil in a large frying pan and cook the onion until soft and translucent, about 5 minutes.
2. Add the remaining vegetables and vegan mince. Stirring occasionally, cook for several more minutes, until the vegetables and mince are cooked through.
3. Add the spices and tomato sauce. Bring to a gentle simmer for 5 minutes, stirring occasionally.
4. Add the beans, stirring and cooking until heated through.
5. Serve with carbs of choice and enjoy!

Savory Steel-Cut Oatmeal

Prep Time: 10 minutes

Cook Time: 30 minutes

Total Time: 40 minutes

Yield: 2-4 servings

INGREDIENTS

- 1 tablespoon olive oil (15ml)
- 1 medium zucchini, finely diced
- 8 oz mushrooms, sliced (225g)
- 4 cups vegetable broth (960ml)
- 3/4 cup steel-cut oats (120g)
- 1/4 cup nutritional yeast flakes (20g)
- 1 cup fresh baby spinach, lightly packed

INSTRUCTIONS

1. Heat oil in a large skillet or wok. Add zucchini and mushrooms and sauté until soft.
2. Add vegetable broth to the sautéed veggies, followed by the oats.
3. While mixing, bring to a rapid boil. Then, reduce heat to low and allow the oats to simmer until tender, 30-45 minutes.
4. Stir in the nutritional yeast and baby spinach. Continue to heat on low until thick & creamy.
5. Transfer to bowls and enjoy!

T-OAT-ALLY SIMILAR!

This recipe is similar to mushroom risotto, but made with steel-cut oats instead of rice.

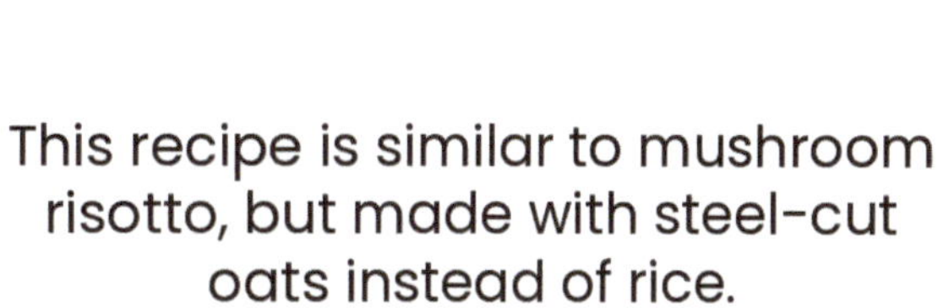

High Protein Lentil Soup

Prep Time: 10 minutes

Cook Time: 20 minutes

Total Time: 30 minutes

Yield: 2-4 servings

INGREDIENTS

- 1 tablespoon olive oil (15ml) *or other neutral oil*
- 1 yellow onion, finely chopped (omit if sensitive to onion)
- 2 large carrots, sliced
- 4 stalks celery, sliced
- 1/2 medium zucchini, sliced
- 15 oz pack vegan mince (400g)
- 2 cups vegetable broth (480ml)
- 2 tablespoons tomato paste (30g)
- 15 oz can crushed tomatoes (400g)
- 2/3 cup dry green lentils (120g)
- Salt, pepper, and additional spices, to taste

spice it up!

Feel free to experiment with different spices and seasonings to give this soup an extra flavor kick! Depending on your sensory preferences, you can keep it simple with salt and pepper, or add distinctive flavors such as turmeric, chili powder, cayenne, paprika, garam masala, etc.

INSTRUCTIONS

1. Heat oil in a large pot or Dutch oven and add onion, carrots, celery, zucchini, and vegan mince. Sauté until soft and fragrant.
2. Add vegetable broth, tomato paste, crushed tomatoes, lentils, and spices. Mix to combine.
3. Bring to a rapid boil, then reduce heat to low. Stirring occasionally, allow soup to simmer until the lentils are cooked through, about 20 minutes.
4. Serve the soup with your choice of carbs! I love adding meal-prepped (sweet) potatoes directly to the soup (page 10), or enjoying it with some fresh bread.

executive functioning tip!

Cooking can feel overwhelming for neurodivergent individuals for a multitude of reasons. Not only do you need to choose what to make, but it requires grocery shopping, navigating kitchen equipment, and clean-up. I love one-pot meals because they minimize the amount of stimulus involved in the process.

Vegan Lentil Loaf

Prep Time: 30 minutes

Cook Time: 1.5 hours

Total Time: 2 hours

Yield: 1 loaf

INGREDIENTS

- 3/4 cup dry green lentils (135g)
- 2 cups vegetable broth (480ml)
- 2 tablespoons ground flaxseed (14g)
- 1/4 cup water (60ml)
- 1 tablespoon olive oil (15ml)
- 1/2 medium onion, chopped (omit if sensitive to onion)
- 2 medium carrots, sliced
- 1 stalk celery, chopped
- 1/2 cup rolled oats (40g)
- 1/3 cup oat flour (40g)
- 1/2 teaspoon ground cumin
- 1/4 teaspoon salt
- 1/4 teaspoon black pepper
- 1/4 cup ketchup or BBQ sauce (60g)

executive functioning tip!

This plant-based "meatloaf" is an excellent source of protein, making it a great base to build a meal around! Simply pair a few slices with starches (such as mashed potatoes or rice, or use bread to make a sandwich), veggies or fruit, and fats (such as butter or gravy) and you've got yourself a satisfying plate in no time!

INSTRUCTIONS

1. Add lentils and vegetable broth to a large pot and bring to a rapid boil. Reduce heat, cover, and simmer for about 40 minutes, stirring occasionally.
2. Once the lentils are done, remove lid and set aside to cool.
3. Preheat oven to 350F/180C. Lightly grease a loaf pan with oil and set aside.
4. In a small bowl, whisk together the flaxseed and water. Set aside for 10 minutes to thicken.
5. Heat oil in a skillet or pan over medium heat. Add onion, carrots, and celery. Sauté vegetables until softened, about 5 minutes.
6. Rinse & drain the cooked lentils and add to a food processor along with the flax mixture, sautéed vegetables, oats, oat flour, and spices.
7. Pulse until a chunky dough forms. Make sure not to overblend, as you want to keep some bits for texture!

8. Press the dough into your prepared loaf pan, and spread the sauce evenly over the top.
9. Place in the center of your preheated oven, and bake for 45-50 minutes. Allow the loaf to cool at least 10 minutes before slicing, as it firms up during this time.
10. Serve with your favorite sides and enjoy!

Low-carb Pumpkin Lasagna

Prep Time: 20 minutes

Cook Time: 25 minutes

Total Time: 45 minutes

Yield: 3-4 servings

INGREDIENTS

ricotta:

- 1/2 cup tahini (120g)
- 7 oz. firm tofu (210g) *use soy-free tofu if necessary*
- 1 tablespoon fresh lemon juice (15ml)
- 2 tablespoons nutritional yeast (10g)
- 1 tablespoon fresh rosemary
- 1 tablespoon fresh thyme
- salt and pepper, to taste

lasagna:

- 1 medium kabocha pumpkin or butternut squash (or a 350g pack of store-bought pumpkin lasagna sheets)
- 1 cup marinara sauce (240g)
- 2 cups baby spinach leaves, loosely packed (50g)
- 1/4 cup fresh basil, loosely packed (10g)
- 3.5 oz vegan mozzarella cheese (100g) *can use regular mozzarella cheese if not dairy-free*

INSTRUCTIONS

1. To make the vegan ricotta, add all ricotta ingredients to a food processor or blender and pulse until smooth. You'll want to blend long enough for it to become creamy, but be careful not to over-blend. We want it to resemble ricotta, not savory yogurt! ;)
2. To make the lasagna, start by preheating the oven to 350F/180C. Lightly grease an 11x7in (27x18cm) oven dish and set aside.
3. Cut the squash in half and remove the seeds and stringy pieces. Cut thin slices lengthwise – these are going to serve as the lasagna sheets! *If using store-bought lasagna sheets, skip this step.*
4. Spread half of the marinara sauce on the prepared oven dish. Top with half of the pumpkin "sheets," followed by half of the vegan ricotta, half of the spinach, and half of the basil.
5. Repeat this process with the remaining ingredients, then top everything with the (vegan) mozzarella.
6. Bake in preheated oven for 25-30 minutes, or until the cheese is melted and the pumpkin is tender.

Spiced Chickpea Pumpkin Curry

Prep Time: 10 minutes

Cook Time: 20 minutes

Total Time: 30 minutes

Yield: 3 bowls

INGREDIENTS

- 2 heaping cups cubed kabocha pumpkin (300g)
- 2 cups water (480ml)
- 1 cup crushed tomatoes (240g)
- 3 tablespoons tomato paste (45g)
- 1/2 tablespoon garam masala
- 1/2 tablespoon curry madras
- 3 tablespoons tahini (45g)
- 15 oz can chickpeas, rinsed and drained (240g drained weight)

sweet potato and butternut squash also work great!

INSTRUCTIONS

1. Add the pumpkin and water to a large pot. Boil for 10-15 minutes or until the pumpkin is fork tender.
2. Add the remaining ingredients. Stirring occasionally, simmer until thick and fragrant.
3. Serve the curry with carbs of choice and enjoy! Pairs excellent with rice, quinoa, or bread :)

10-minute Tofu Curry

Prep Time: 5 minutes

Cook Time: 5 minutes

Total Time: 10 minutes

Yield: 3-4 servings

single serve + just 3 ingredients!

Depending on your heat preference, go for a mild, medium, or hot curry paste!

INGREDIENTS

- 16 oz pack firm tofu (450g) *use soy-free tofu if necessary*
- 1 cup full-fat coconut milk (240ml)
- 2 tablespoons curry paste (30g)

INSTRUCTIONS

1. To make the tofu, start by cutting the block into cubes and coating with a bit of oil. Then, either pan-fry or air-fry at 375F/190C until crispy and golden (5-7 minutes).
2. While the tofu is cooking, heat coconut milk in a small saucepan over medium heat.
3. Once the coconut milk starts to bubble, whisk in the curry paste. Mix until you have a smooth sauce.
4. Add the cooked tofu, and serve with carbs and veggies of choice!

3-ingredient Pizza Bagels

Prep Time: 5 minutes

Cook Time: 5 minutes

Total Time: 10 minutes

Yield: 1 serving

INGREDIENTS

- 1 large bagel
- 1/4 cup tomato sauce (60g)
- 1 slice (vegan) cheese or a few tablespoons shredded (vegan) cheese (30g)
- Vegetables and other toppings, as desired (fresh basil, spinach, mushrooms, and peppers are some of my favorites!)

INSTRUCTIONS

1. Slice bagel in half and spread tomato sauce evenly over the two halves.
2. Top with cheese and any additional toppings.
3. Air-fry at 350F/180C for 5 minutes, or bake in a preheated oven at the same temperature for 8-10 minutes.
4. Allow to cool slightly, then enjoy!

no bagels? no problem!

If you don't have bagels on hand, you can use two slices of your favorite bread instead!

African-inspired Veggie Stew

Prep Time: 10 minutes

Cook Time: 20 minutes

Total Time: 30 minutes

Yield: 3 bowls

INGREDIENTS

- 2 tablespoons olive oil (30ml)
- 1/2 yellow onion, chopped*
- 3 scallions, chopped*

*sensitive to onions? omit them!

- 1 red bell pepper, diced
- 1 eggplant, cubed
- 1 cup broccoli florets (90g)
- 3/4 cup sliced mushrooms (65g)
- 1 cup chopped kale *such as Cavolo Nero* (65g)
- 3 cups vegetable broth (720ml)
- 2 tablespoons tomato paste (30g)
- 15 oz can diced tomatoes (400g)
- 1/2 cup sunflower seed butter (120g) (p. 16)
- 15 oz can chickpeas, rinsed and drained (240g drained weight)

INSTRUCTIONS

1. Heat oil in a large pot or Dutch oven. Add all your veggies and sauté until wilted and fragrant.
2. Add vegetable broth, tomato paste, canned tomatoes, and sunflower seed butter. Mix to combine.
3. Bring to a gentle boil, stirring continuously.
4. Add chickpeas, and continue to heat on low for a few more minutes.
5. Transfer to bowls and enjoy!

White Bean Shakshuka

Prep Time: 10 minutes

Cook Time: 20 minutes

Total Time: 30 minutes

Yield: 2-3 servings

INGREDIENTS

- 2 tablespoons olive oil (30ml)
- 1 yellow onion, finely chopped (omit if sensitive)
- 1 cup chopped kale (65g)
- 28 oz canned crushed tomatoes (800g)
- 1 teaspoon smoked paprika
- 1 teaspoon ground cumin
- 1 teaspoon dried oregano
- salt and pepper, to taste
- 15 oz can cannellini beans, rinsed and drained (240g drained weight)

INSTRUCTIONS

1. Heat oil in a skillet over medium heat. Add the onion and sauté until translucent.
2. Add the kale and cook until wilted down.
3. Add the tomatoes and spices, stirring well to combine. Allow the sauce to come to a simmer.
4. Add beans and cook until heated through.
5. Serve and enjoy! This dish pairs excellent with bread.

What is Shakshuka?

Traditional Shakshuka is made up of saucy tomatoes, onions, and other vegetables, with eggs cracked into the mix. In this 100% plant-based recipe, we use white beans instead of eggs.

SWEETS

Blueberry Crumble Muffins

Prep Time: 15 minutes

Cook Time: 20 minutes

Total Time: 35 minutes

Yield: 6 muffins

INGREDIENTS

- 2 tablespoons ground flaxseed (14g) ⬅ ground chia seed
- 1/3 cup water (80ml)
- 1/2 cup applesauce (120g)
- 1/2 cup nut/seed butter (120g)
- 1/4 cup maple syrup (60ml) ⬅ other sticky sweetener such as agave
- 1 teaspoon vanilla extract
- 1/4 teaspoon salt
- 1 teaspoon baking soda
- 3/4 cup tigernut flour (84g) ⬅ almond flour if not nut-free
- 1/4 cup coconut flour (28g)
- 1/2 cup arrowroot starch (72g) ⬅ cornstarch
- 1 cup fresh blueberries (120g) ⬅ other fruit

Substitution tips!

This recipe requires quite a few different ingredients that aren't always in everyone's pantry, so no worries – you can easily substitute most of the ingredients! See above arrows for each specific substitution.

INSTRUCTIONS

1. Preheat oven to 350F/180C and prepare 6 cups of a muffin tin either by greasing lightly with coconut oil or cooking spray OR by lining with 6 muffin cups.
2. In a large mixing bowl, whisk together the ground flaxseed and water. Allow to sit for 5-10 minutes to thicken.
3. Add the applesauce, nut/seed butter, maple syrup, vanilla, salt, and baking soda. Whisk well.
4. Mix in the flours until well combined and you have a smooth batter.
5. Gently fold in the blueberries, then distribute batter evenly over the muffin cups.
6. Bake muffins in preheated oven for 18-22 minutes, or until golden brown and a toothpick inserted in the center of one of the muffins comes out clean.
7. Allow to cool for at least 30 minutes before removing from the tin, as muffins will be delicate!
8. Store the muffins covered on the countertop for 2 days, or keep in the fridge or freezer for longer.

Carrot Loaf Cake

Prep Time: 15 minutes

Cook Time: 45 minutes

Total Time: 1 hour

Yield: 8-10 slices

INGREDIENTS

- 2 tablespoons ground flaxseed (14g)
- 1/3 cup water (80ml)
- 2/3 cup applesauce (160g)
- 1/4 cup maple syrup (60ml)
- 1/4 cup milk of choice (60ml)
- 3 tbsp coconut oil, melted (45g)
- 1 teaspoon vanilla extract
- 1/4 teaspoon salt
- 1 teaspoon cinnamon
- 1 pinch nutmeg
- 1 pinch ginger
- 1 pinch cloves
- 1 teaspoon baking powder
- 1 teaspoon baking soda
- 1 cup tigernut flour (112g)
- 1 cup gluten-free all-purpose flour (120g)
- 1 1/2 cups grated carrot (120g)

Substitution tips!

This recipe requires quite a few different ingredients that aren't always in everyone's pantry, so no worries! See the Ingredients & Equipment page at the beginning of this book for alternatives.

INSTRUCTIONS

1. Preheat oven to 350F/180C. Lightly grease a loaf pan and line with parchment paper. Set aside.
2. In a large mixing bowl, whisk together the ground flaxseed and water. Allow to sit for 5-10 minutes to thicken.
3. Add applesauce, maple syrup, milk, coconut oil, vanilla, salt, spices, baking powder, and baking soda. Whisk well to combine.
4. Fold in the flours and grated carrot until well mixed. The batter should be thick, yet pourable.
5. Pour batter into the prepared loaf pan and bake in preheated oven until a toothpick inserted in the center comes out clean, approximately 40-50 minutes.
6. Allow the loaf to cool completely before removing from pan and frosting.

Looking for an easy frosting recipe?

See my recipe for Cocoyogo
Frosting on the next page!

Cocoyogo Frosting

Prep Time: 5 minutes

Total Time: 5 minutes

Yield: ~1 cup (280g)

INGREDIENTS

- 1 cup plain Greek-style coconut yogurt (240g)
- 2 tablespoons maple syrup (30ml)
- 1 teaspoon vanilla extract
- 2 tablespoons GF all-purpose flour (15g) *or cornstarch*

INSTRUCTIONS

1. Add all ingredients to a bowl and mix using an electric mixer or hand whisk.
2. Use as desired and store any remaining frosting in an airtight container in the fridge.

How can I use this frosting?

You can use this easy frosting recipe to dazzle up any dish, including oats, cakes, and more! It's an essential topper of my Carrot Loaf Cake and Lemon Poppyseed Loaf Cake!

Lemon Poppyseed Loaf Cake

Prep Time: 15 minutes

Cook Time: 45 minutes

Total Time: 1 hour

Yield: 8-10 slices

INGREDIENTS

- 1/2 cup milk of choice (120ml)
- Juice + zest of 1 lemon
- 1/2 cup applesauce (120g)
- 1/2 cup sugar (110g)
- 3 tablespoons coconut oil, melted (45g)
- 1 teaspoon vanilla extract
- 1/4 teaspoon salt
- 1 teaspoon baking powder
- 1 teaspoon baking soda
- 1 cup tigernut flour (112g)
- 1 cup gluten-free all-purpose flour (120g)
- 1 tablespoon poppy seeds (12g)
- 1x Cocoyogo Frosting recipe (p. 70)

INSTRUCTIONS

1. Preheat oven to 350F/180C. Lightly grease a loaf pan and line with parchment paper. Set aside.
2. In a large mixing bowl, whisk together all ingredients except for the flours and poppy seeds (and frosting obviously!).
3. Fold in the flours and poppy seeds.
4. Pour batter into your prepared loaf pan and bake in preheated oven until a toothpick inserted in the center comes out clean, approximately 40-50 minutes.
5. Cool completely before removing from pan and frosting.

Sweet Potato Brownies

Prep Time: 10 minutes

Cook Time: 20 minutes

Total Time: 30 minutes

Yield: 8 brownies

INGREDIENTS

- 1 cup baked and mashed sweet potato (240g)
- 1/2 cup nut/seed butter (120g)
- 1/3 cup cocoa powder (30g)
- 2 tablespoons maple syrup (30ml)
- 1/4 teaspoon salt

see my recipe for Perfectly Baked Sweet Potatoes on page 10!

INSTRUCTIONS

1. Preheat oven to 350F/180C. Lightly grease a loaf pan with coconut oil or cooking spray and line with parchment paper. Set aside.
2. Add all ingredients to a blender or food processor. Blend on HIGH until you have a thick, yet smooth batter.
3. Transfer batter to your greased loaf pan (batter will be thick!) and bake for 20-25 minutes, or until toothpick inserted in the center of the loaf comes out clean.
4. Allow the brownies to cool completely before slicing.

executive functioning tip!

Always keep a batch of brownies or other goodies in your freezer! Simply slice and freeze brownies in an airtight container and you'll have a nutritious snack ready to go!

Fig Newton Bars

Prep Time: 15 minutes

Cook Time: 30 minutes

Total Time: 45 minutes

Yield: 8 bars

INGREDIENTS

Filling:
- 1 1/2 cups dried figs (240g)
- 1/2 teaspoon ground cinnamon
- 1/4 cup milk of choice (60ml)

Crust:
- 1 3/4 cups tigernut flour (196g)
- 1/4 cup coconut flour (28g)
- 2 tablespoons ground flaxseed (14g)
- 1 teaspoon baking powder
- 1/2 teaspoon baking soda
- 3/4 cup applesauce (180g)

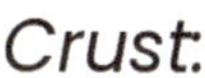

INSTRUCTIONS

1. Preheat oven to 350F/180C. Lightly grease a loaf pan and line with parchment paper.
2. In a food processor, blend the filling ingredients until you have a thick, yet smooth paste. Set aside.
3. In a large bowl, mix together the crust ingredients until a thick dough forms.
4. Press half of the crust mixture evenly in the loaf pan.
5. Spread the filling on top, then add the rest of the crust on top of that.
6. Bake for approximately 30 minutes and allow to cool completely before slicing.

Funfetti Protein Bars

Prep Time: 15 minutes

Total Time: 15 minutes

Yield: 8 bars

INGREDIENTS

- 1 cup pitted dates (175g)
- 1/2 cup nut/seed butter (120g)
- 4 scoops vegan vanilla protein powder (50g)
- 1/4 cup coconut flour (28g)
- 1/4 teaspoon salt *omit if nut/seed butter is salted*
- 1/3 cup warm water (80ml)
- 2 tablespoons sprinkles (30g) *or chocolate chips*

INSTRUCTIONS

1. Prepare a loaf pan by greasing lightly with coconut oil or cooking spray and lining with parchment paper. Set aside.
2. Add all ingredients except sprinkles to a food processor, blending until you have a thick, yet smooth batter.
3. Press dough into prepared loaf pan and top with sprinkles (or chocolate chips). Place in freezer for 30 minutes to set, then slice into bars and enjoy!

WHY MAKE YOUR OWN PROTEIN BARS?

Protein bars are an excellent snack because they are packed with protein, fiber, and healthy fats. However, they are often filled with additional ingredients that don't always agree with sensitive bodies, which is why making them at home is such a great option! Plus, you get to customize the flavors – which is always fun!

CELEBRATE GOOD TIMES, COME ON!

Can you name that song? In all seriousness though, you don't need to wait until there's a party to make these bars. Your LIFE is a party, so it's always a good time to dance in the kitchen!

White Chocolate Tigernut Muffins

Prep Time: 15 minutes

Cook Time: 15 minutes

Total Time: 30 minutes

Yield: 6 muffins

INGREDIENTS

- 1/2 cup plantain flour (60g)
- 1/4 cup coconut flour (28g)
- 1/4 cup tigernut flour (28g) ← almond flour if not nut-free
- 2 scoops vegan vanilla protein powder (25g-30g)
- 1 tablespoon ground chia seeds (6g) ← ground flaxseed
- 1 teaspoon baking powder
- 1/2 teaspoon baking soda
- 1/3 cup coconut oil, melted (80g) ← butter or neutral oil
- 1/3 cup maple syrup (80ml) ← other sticky sweetener
- 1/2 cup milk of choice (120ml)
- 1/4 cup chopped tiger nuts (28g) *or macadamia nuts if not nut-free*
- 50g chopped white chocolate or chocolate chips

Substitution tips!

As in several of my other recipes, the arrows indicate easy swaps. This recipe for White Chocolate Tigernut Muffins is a nut-free spin on the classic White Chocolate Macadamia Nut Muffins, so if you're not nut-free, feel free to use chopped macadamia nuts instead of tiger nuts.

INSTRUCTIONS

1. Preheat oven to 350F/180C and prepare a muffin tin either by greasing lightly with coconut oil or cooking spray OR by lining with 6 muffin cups.
2. In a mixing bowl, whisk together the dry ingredients: plantain flour, coconut flour, tigernut flour, protein powder, chia seeds, baking powder and baking soda.
3. Add the coconut oil, maple syrup, and milk of choice. Mix well and allow to sit for 5-7 minutes to thicken.
4. Gently fold in chopped tiger nuts and white chocolate. Distribute batter evenly over the muffin cups.
5. Bake in preheated oven for 15-18 minutes, or until a toothpick inserted in the center of a muffin comes out clean.
6. Allow to cool for at least 15 minutes and enjoy!

DID YOU KNOW?

Cacao butter is one of the main ingredients in white chocolate. It's high in omega-3 fatty acids, which support cognitive function!

Chocolate Brownie Balls

Prep Time: 15 minutes

Total Time: 15 minutes

Yield: 8 balls

INGREDIENTS

- 1 cup pitted dates (175g)
- 1/2 cup tigernut flour (56g)
- 1/3 cup cocoa powder (30g)

INSTRUCTIONS

1. Add all ingredients to a food processor and pulse/blend until a dough forms.
2. Roll into balls and enjoy!

2 easy swaps!

- No dates? Use any other dried fruit!
- Not nut-free? Use almond flour instead of tigernut!

Carrot Cake Bliss Balls

Prep Time: 15 minutes

Total Time: 15 minutes

Yield: 8 balls

INGREDIENTS

- 1 cup pitted dates (175g) *or raisins*
- 1/2 cup nuts or seeds (60g)
- 1/4 cup shredded coconut (25g)
- 1/2 cup shredded carrot (40g)
- 1 teaspoon ground cinnamon
- 1 pinch ground ginger
- 1 pinch ground nutmeg
- 1 pinch salt

INSTRUCTIONS

1. Add all ingredients to a food processor and pulse/blend until a dough forms.
2. Roll into balls and enjoy!

If you're not nut-free, I recommend using walnuts or pecans. If you are nut-free, use sunflower or pumpkin seeds!

Chickpea Chocolate Chip Cookies

Prep Time: 15 minutes

Cook Time: 10 minutes

Total Time: 25 minutes

Yield: 8 cookies

INGREDIENTS

- 1 cup cooked chickpeas (120g)
- 1 cup pitted dates (175g) ← any dried fruit will do!
- 2 tablespoons tahini (30g) ← can sub nut/seed butter of choice
- 1/2 teaspoon baking powder
- 1/2 teaspoon vanilla extract
- 2 scoops vegan vanilla protein powder (25g-30g)
- 1/4 cup milk of choice (60ml) *+ more, if necessary*
- 8 chocolate buttons *or squares of homemade dark chocolate (p. 18)*

chickpeas + digestion

Like most legumes, chickpeas are high in fiber and saccharides, a type of sugar that is not digested. This can result in bloating, gas, and cramping, which can be especially difficult to cope with when you're highly sensitive. If you are sensitive to chickpeas, simply enjoy the legume in small amounts (such as a few of these cookies!). You don't have to completely cut them out, because life isn't that black and white!

INSTRUCTIONS

1. Preheat oven to 350F/180C and line a baking tray with a silicone baking mat, parchment paper, or grease lightly with butter or oil.
2. Add all ingredients except for chocolate to a food processor or blender, and blend until a thick ball of dough forms. If the dough is too crumbly, add additional splashes of milk in increments, blending and adding more milk until you have a thick dough.
3. Form the dough into 8 balls, then lightly press each ball down onto the prepared baking tray.
4. Top each cookie with a chocolate button and bake in preheated oven until golden brown, about 10-12 minutes.
5. Allow to cool slightly and enjoy!

pair them with
some dairy-
free milk!

WHAT IS TIGERNUT FLOUR?

Tigernut flour is made from ground tiger nuts. Contrary to its name, the tiger nut is not actually a nut. Tiger nuts are grouped in the same family as the root vegetables, so think potatoes or sweet potatoes! The name "tiger nut" comes from the tuber's nutty taste and stripes on its exterior.

Tiger nuts are very high in fiber, as well as several vitamins and minerals. Perhaps, the most significant nutritional aspect of the tiger nut, however, is that it consists almost solely of resistant starch! Resistant starch is a starch that is resisted by the digestive system, and thus moves into our gut to feed our good bacteria. Tiger nuts are a natural prebiotic, which is a type of plant fiber that feeds the probiotics in your gut. A healthy and happy tummy starts with healthy and happy bacteria, which directly impacts your mental health for the better, too!

WHAT DO YOU THINK?

Thank you so much for buying my book! It would mean the world to me if you could take two minutes to leave a review on Amazon and Goodreads. Your words inspire other people to nourish their neurodiversity!

With love and gratitude,

Liv

READ MORE

Rainbow Girl: A Memoir of Autism and Anorexia

How to Beat Extreme Hunger: Find Food Freedom Without Losing Control

Be the first!
Join the Liv Label Free family and be the first to receive updates on Livia's latest books and content:
www.livlabelfree.com/join

ABOUT THE AUTHOR

LIVIA SARA is an autism advocate and eating disorder survivor that now helps others overcome their own mental barriers through her courses and coaching programs. She is the author of the blog livlabelfree.com and the host of the Liv Label Free Podcast. Livia is a lifelong learner that loves listening to audiobooks, going on walks, and reading the latest science on all things neurodiversity and eating disorders!

www.livlabelfree.com
@livlabelfree